LEARN TO WRITE LETTERS

THIS BOOK BELONGS TO:
_____
_____

OVER THE MOON
PUBLISHING

Copyright © 2024 Over the moon publishing

All rights reserved.

No part of this publication may be reproduced, distributed or transmitted in any form or by any means including photocopying, recording, or other electronic mechanical methods, without the prior written permission of the publisher, except in the case of brief quotations embodied in critical reviews and certain other noncommercial uses permitted by copyright law.

To join our mailing list and see other titles available

Website: www.captaintimpublishing.com

Email: info@captaintimpublishing.com

Trace it and color it	Circle it
	F T Y A
	A E U P
	Q V A G

Trace it and write it

Color the picture and fill in the missing letter

_pple

_lligator

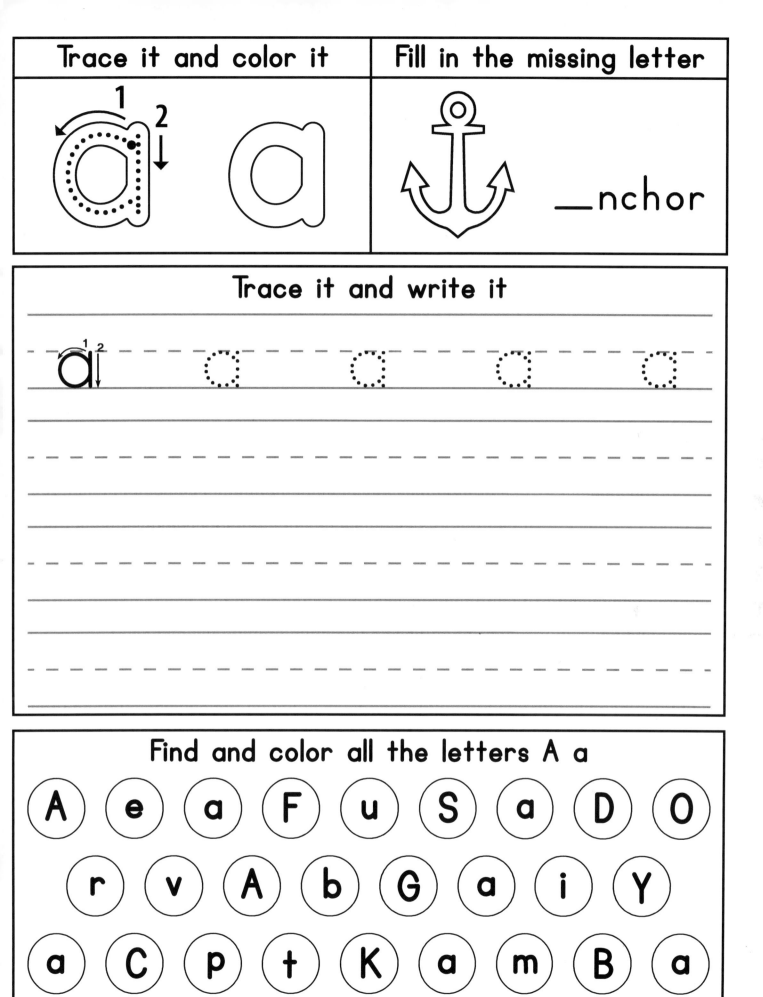

Trace it and color it	Circle it
B B	C B A B B E B D S B B T

Trace it and write it

B B B B B

Color the picture and fill in the missing letter

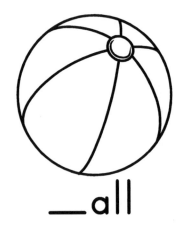

_all

_ook

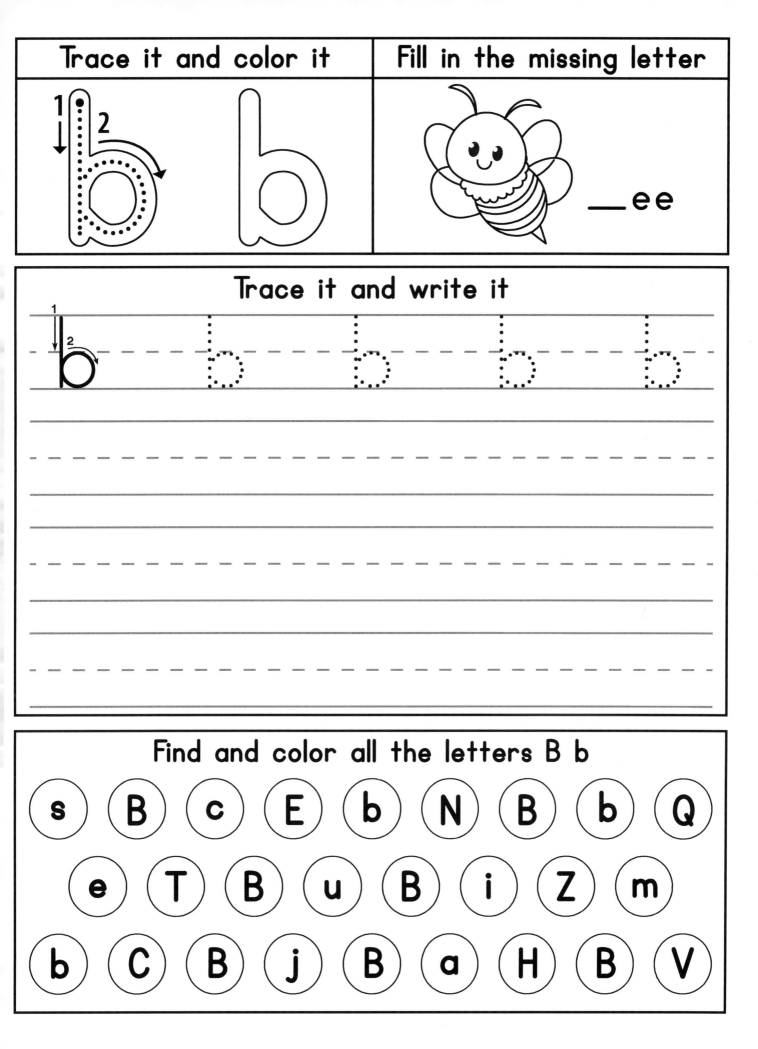

Trace it and color it	Circle it
C C	C I C O A C P C C B C E

Trace it and write it

C C C C C C

Color the picture and fill in the missing letter

_ar

_arrot

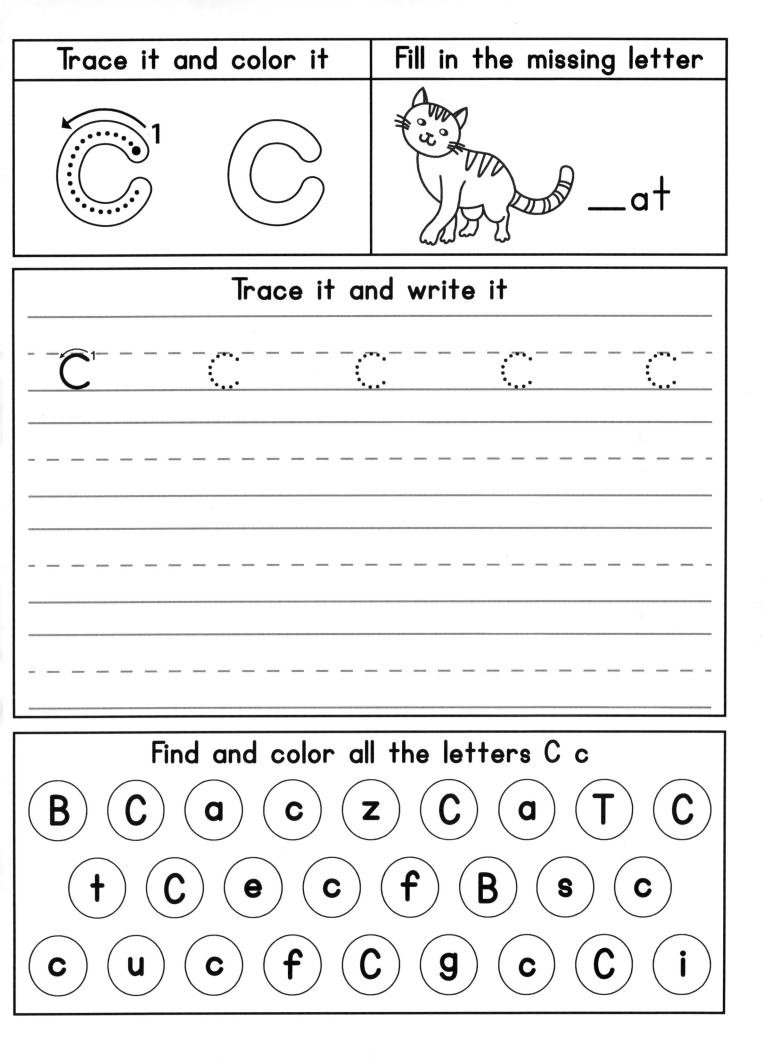

Trace it and color it

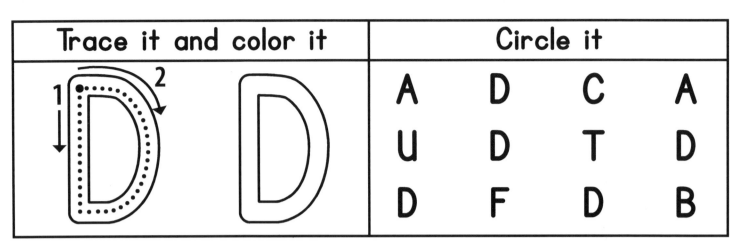

Circle it

A	D	C	A
U	D	T	D
D	F	D	B

Trace it and write it

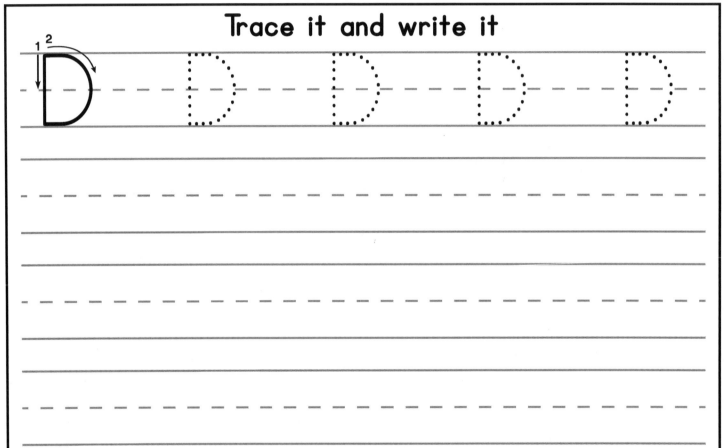

Color the picture and fill in the missing letter

__rum

__ragon

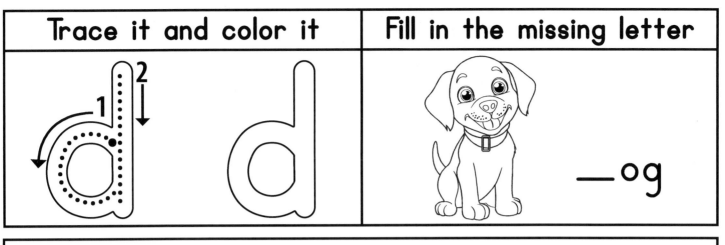
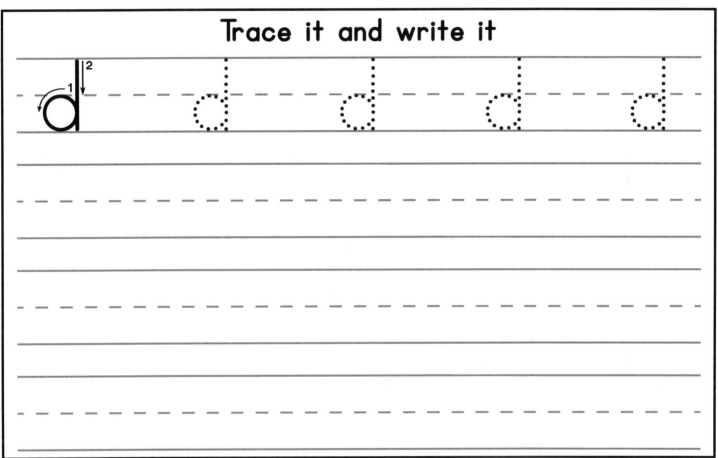
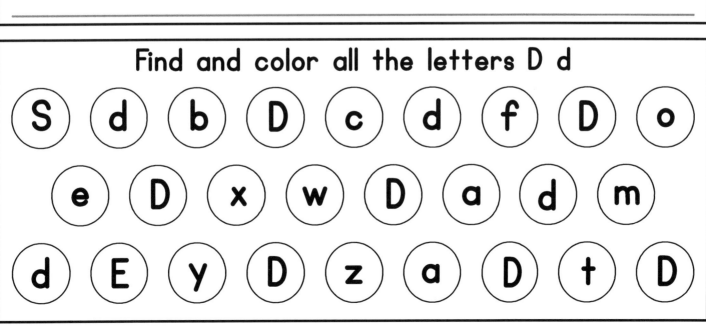

Trace it and color it	Circle it
E E	B E C S A R E E E E Y T

Trace it and write it

E E E E E

Color the picture and fill in the missing letter

___lephant   ___lbow

Trace it and color it	Circle it
	A W F T F P O F L F F K

Trace it and write it

Color the picture and fill in the missing letter

__lower   __lag

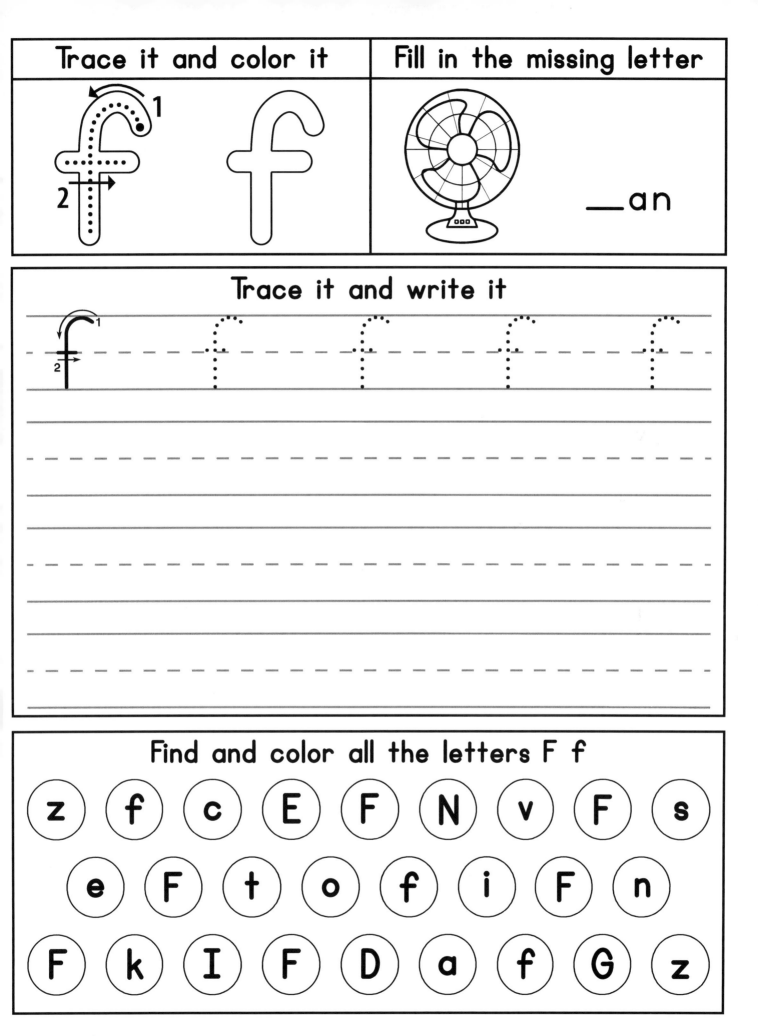

Trace it and color it	Circle it
	G H G F C G A G E G G B

Trace it and write it

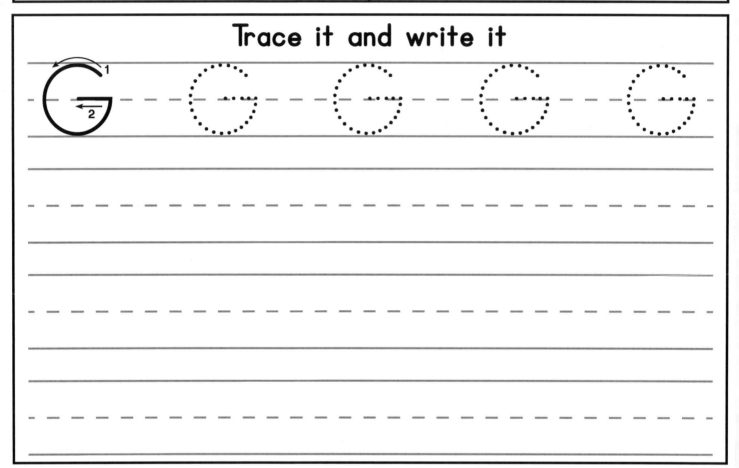

Color the picture and fill in the missing letter

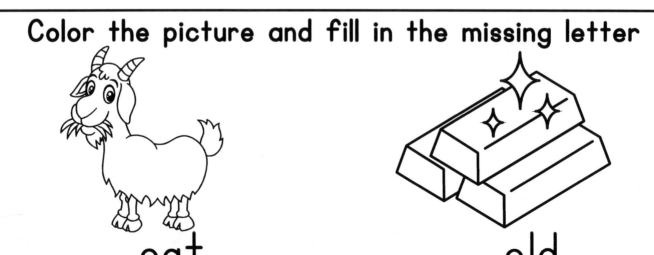

_oat   _old

Trace it and color it	Circle it
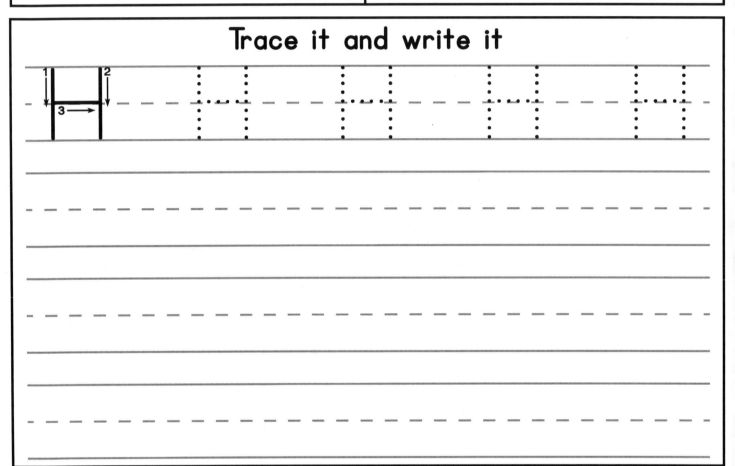	H A H Z C H X H H V H E

Trace it and write it

Color the picture and fill in the missing letter

_ouse

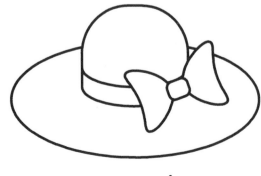
_at

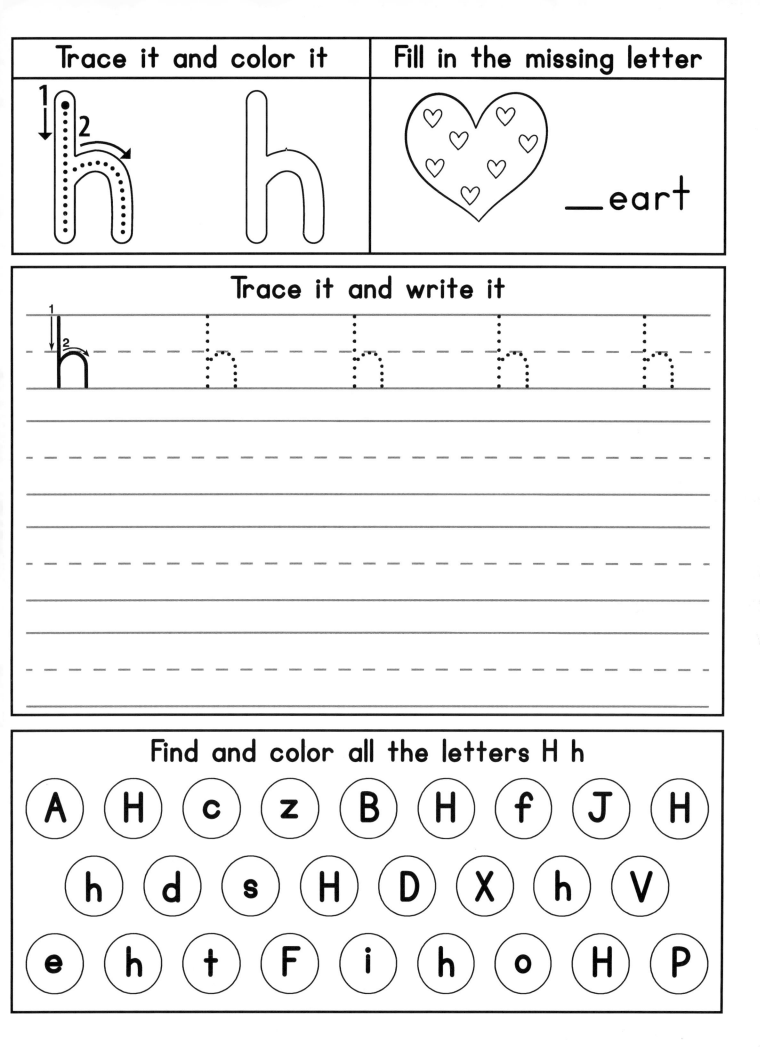

Trace it and color it	Circle it
	I B I N
	L M I N
	I I K J

Trace it and write it

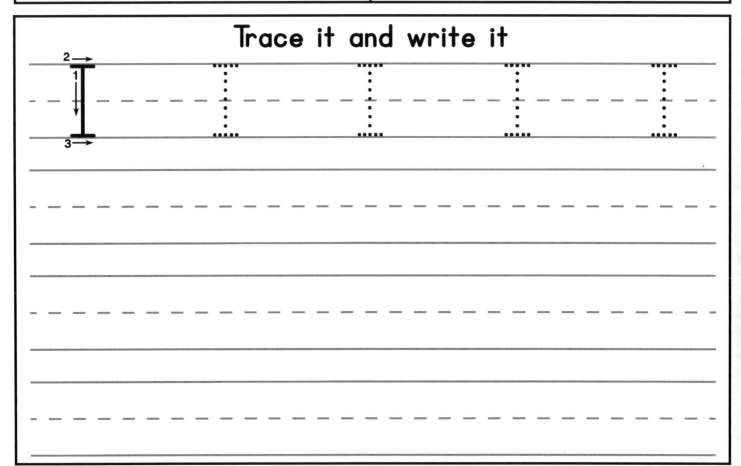

Color the picture and fill in the missing letter

__nk

__gloo

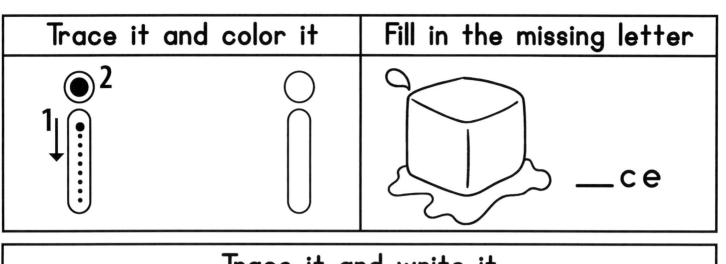

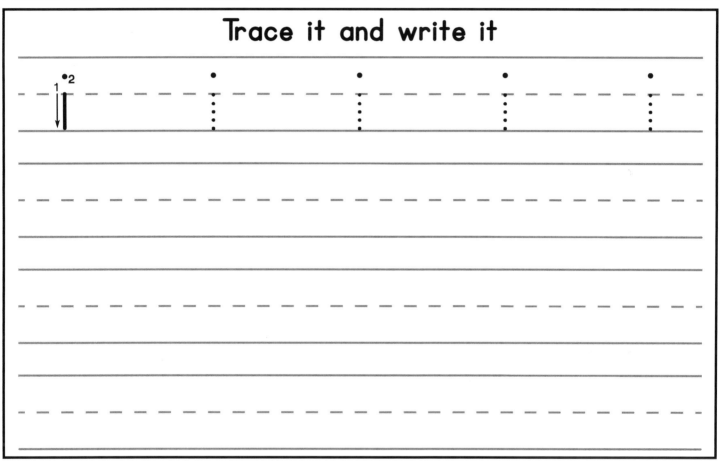

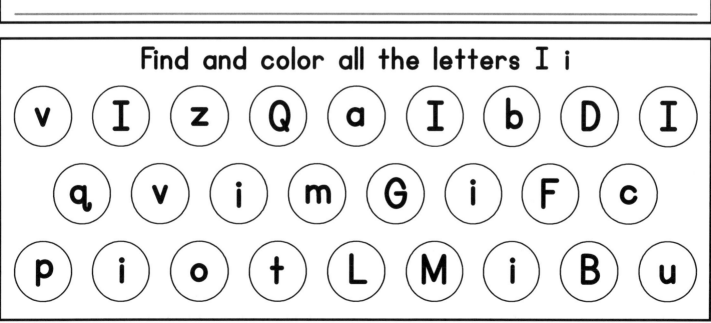

Trace it and color it	Circle it
	J H J G
	D J F J
	S A J Q

Trace it and write it

Color the picture and fill in the missing letter

__uice   __elly

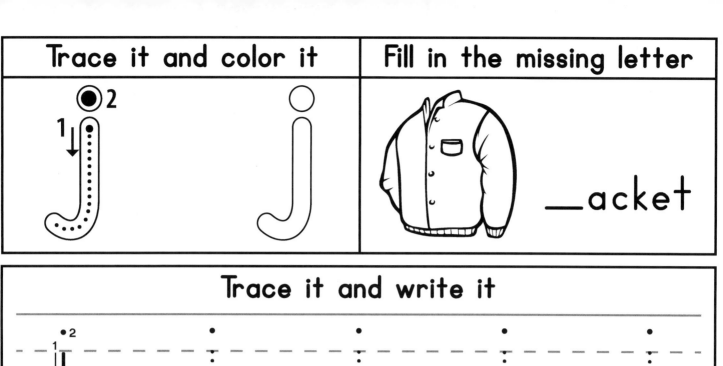
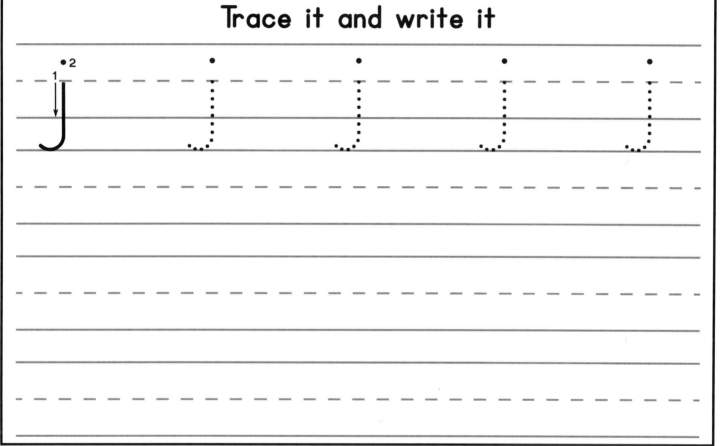
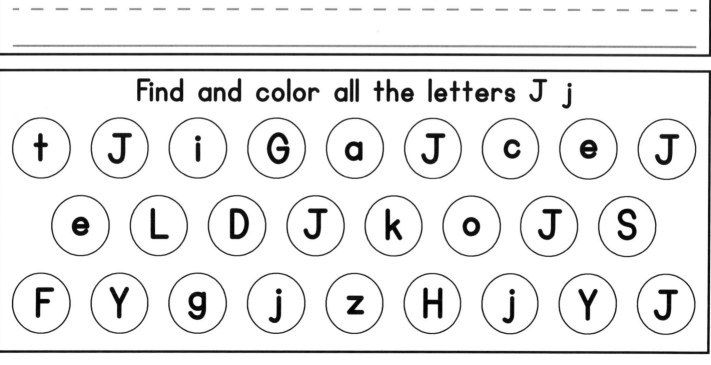

Trace it and color it	Circle it
K K	W E K K R K T Y K I K U

Trace it and write it

K K K K K

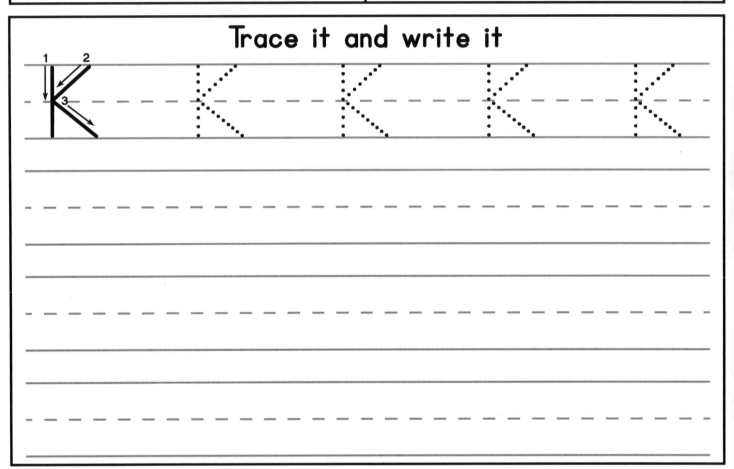

Color the picture and fill in the missing letter

__ite   __angaroo

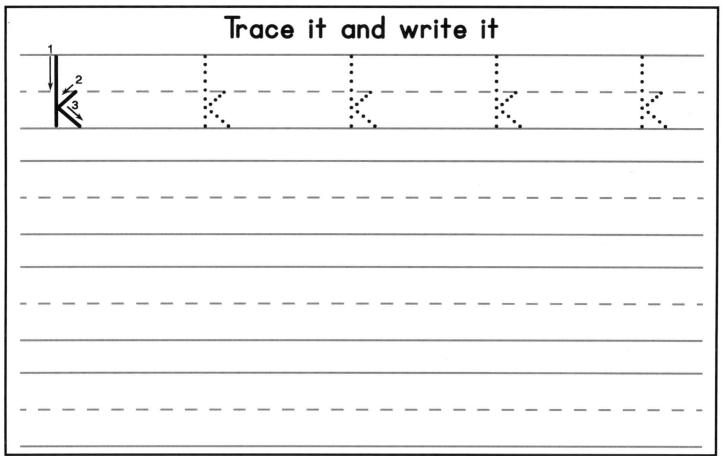

Trace it and color it	Circle it
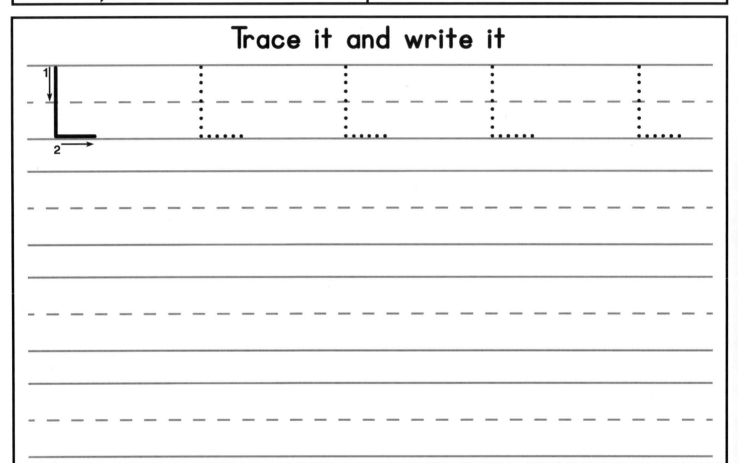	O L P L H J L K L F D L

Trace it and write it

Color the picture and fill in the missing letter

_ion

_emon

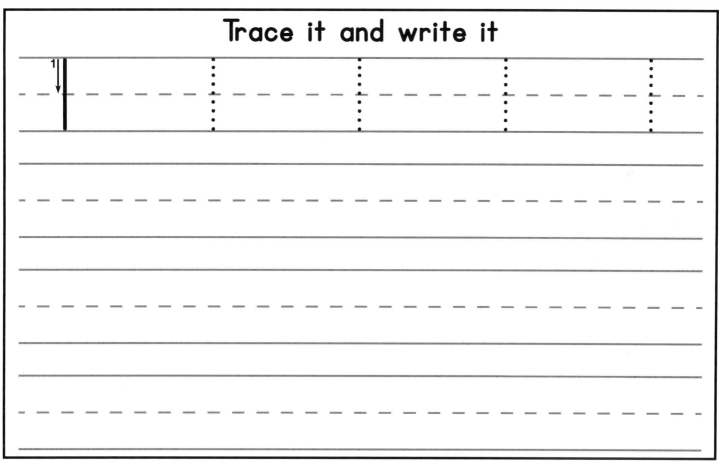

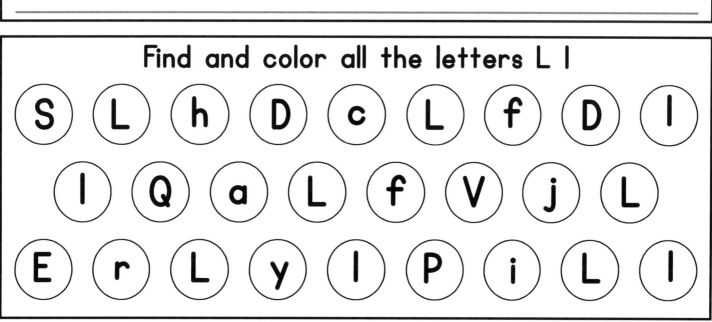

Trace it and color it	Circle it
	M L M K B M N M M C M A

Trace it and write it

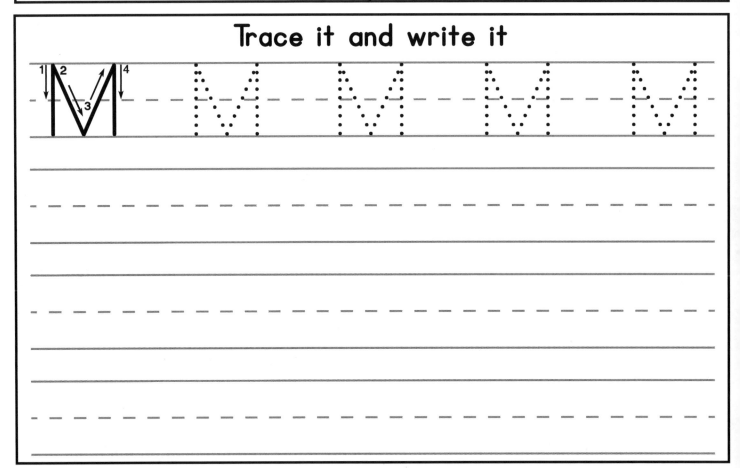

Color the picture and fill in the missing letter

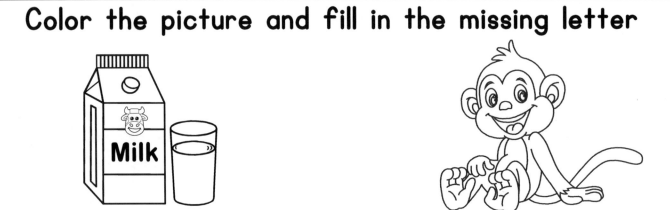

_ilk   _onkey

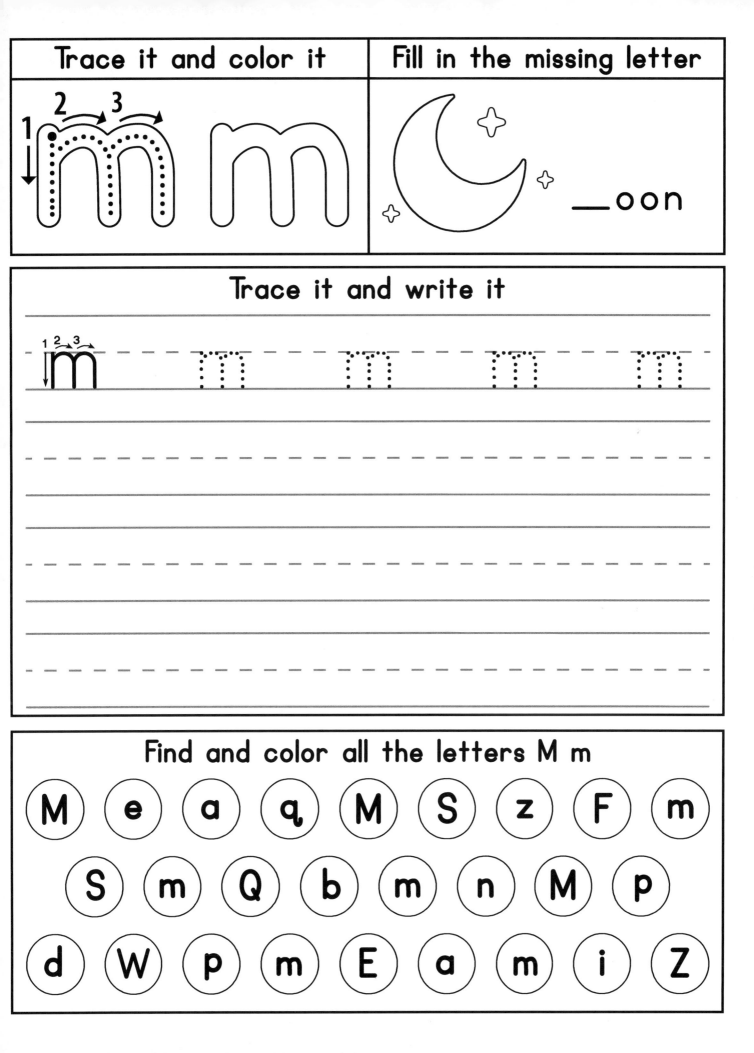

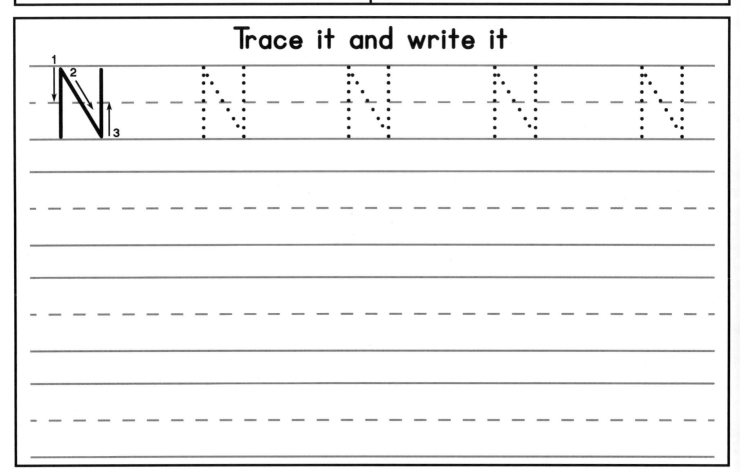

Color the picture and fill in the missing letter

__urse

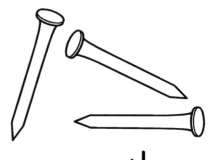

__ail

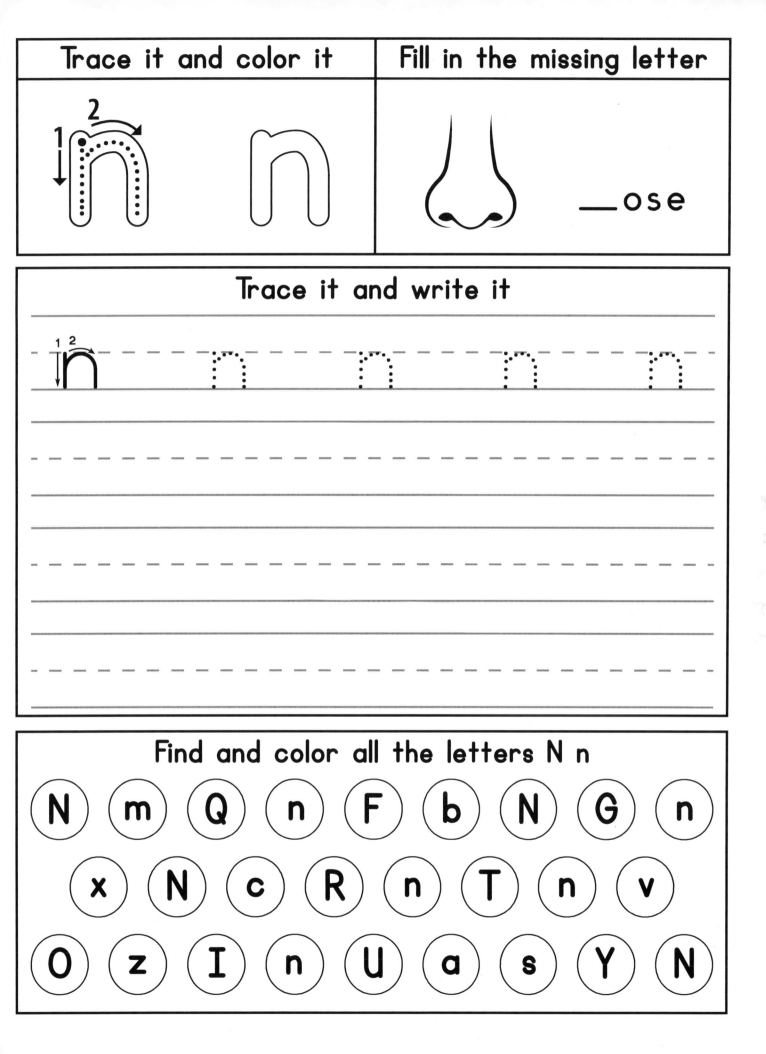

Trace it and color it

O O

Circle it

A	O	Q	O
D	F	O	O
O	O	E	W

Trace it and write it

O O O O O

Color the picture and fill in the missing letter

_ctopus

_range

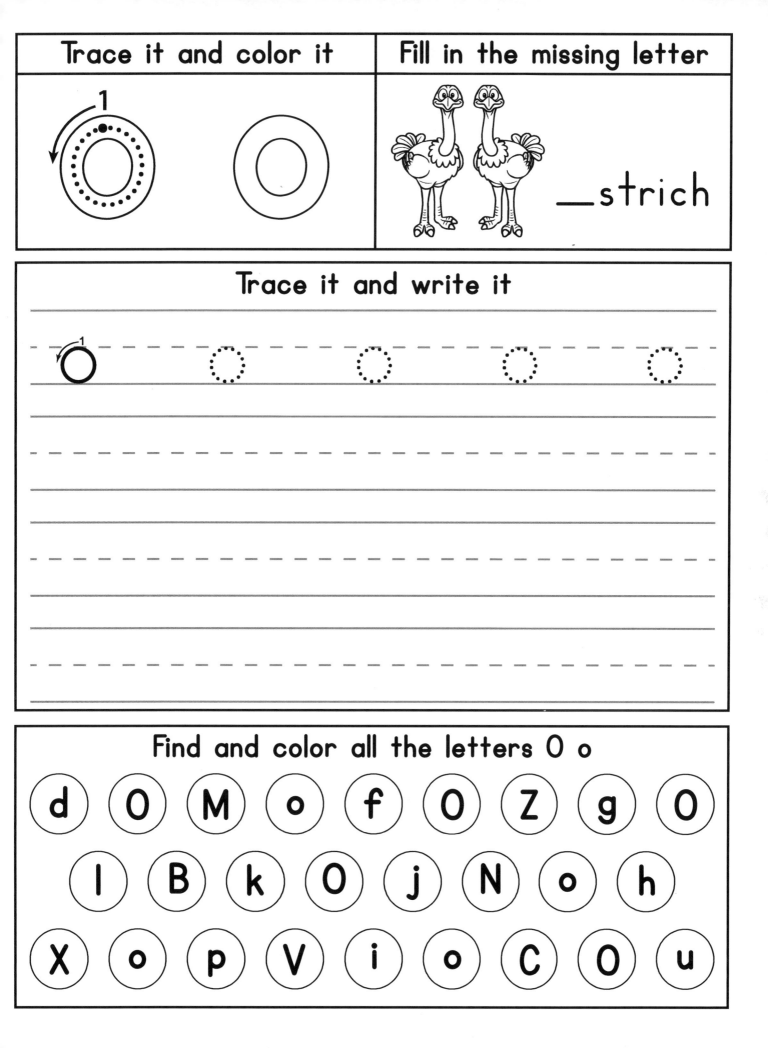

Trace it and color it	Circle it
P P	E R P T U P Y P P C P N

Trace it and write it

P P P P P P

Color the picture and fill in the missing letter

__izza

__ig

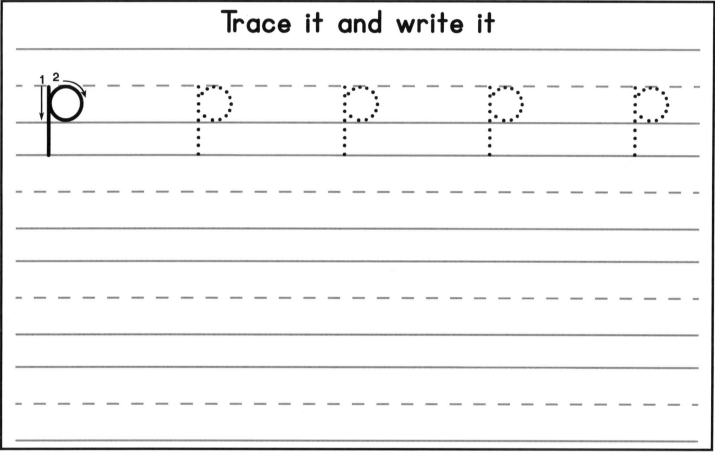
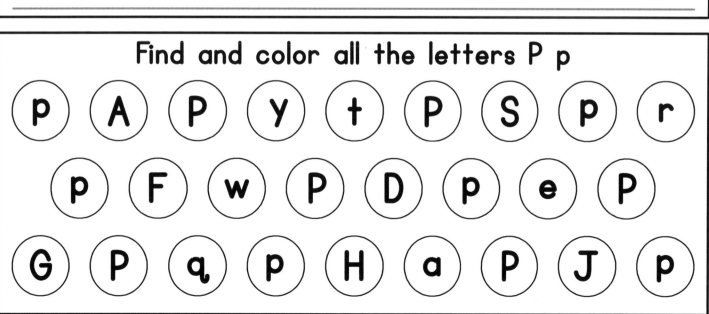

Trace it and color it	Circle it
Q Q	W Q E R Q Y Q T Q U I Q

Trace it and write it

Q Q Q Q Q

Color the picture and fill in the missing letter

_ueen

_uilt

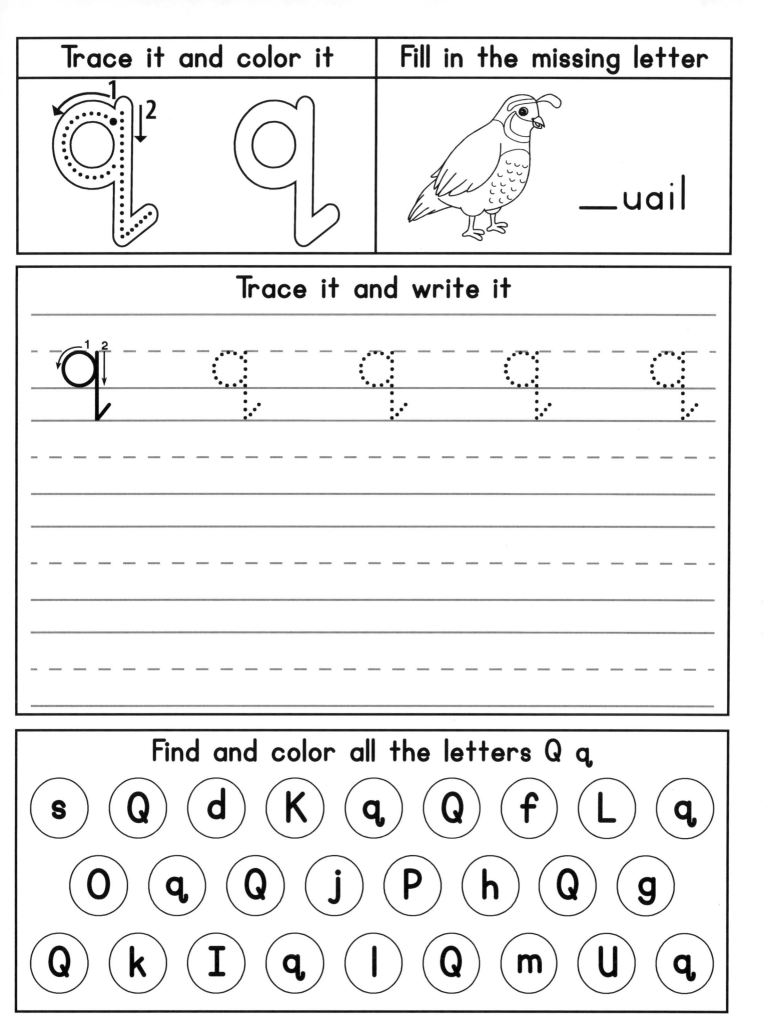

Trace it and color it

R R

Circle it

O	R	P	R
R	K	R	L
F	R	D	R

Trace it and write it

R R R R R

Color the picture and fill in the missing letter

_abbit

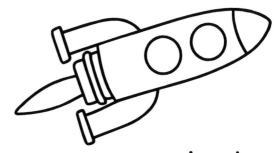
_ocket

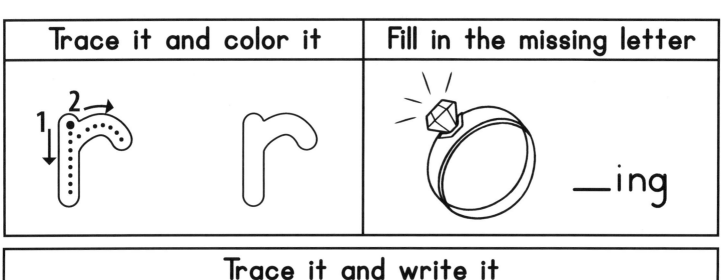

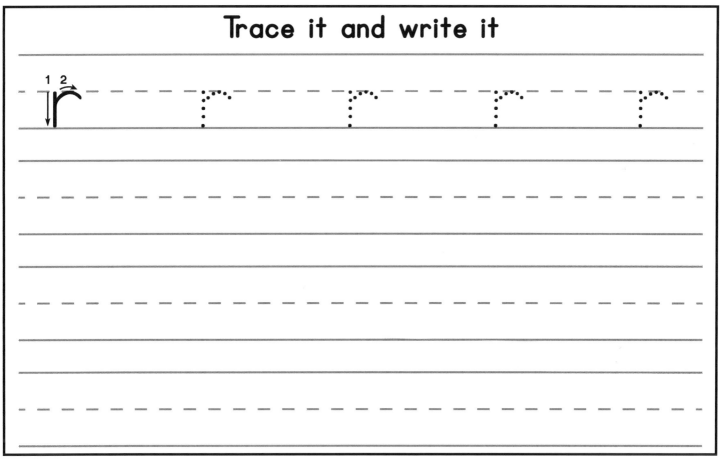

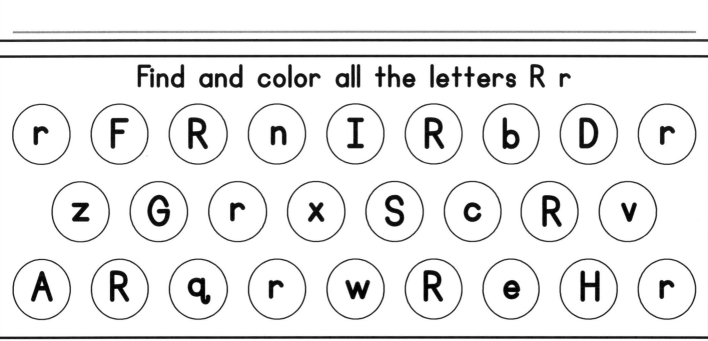

Trace it and color it	Circle it
S S	A F S S H S J S S L S N

Trace it and write it

S S S S S

Color the picture and fill in the missing letter

_un

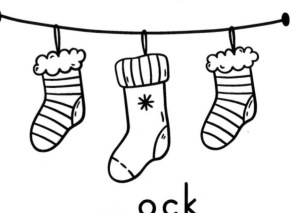

_ock

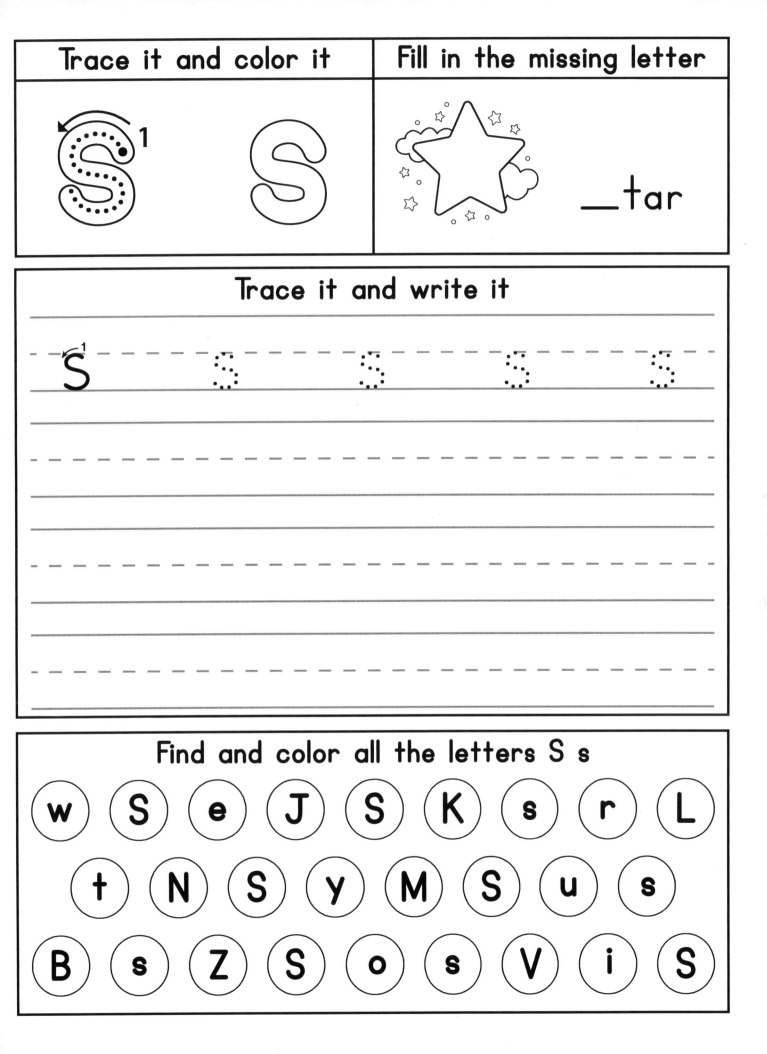

Trace it and color it	Circle it
	T Y T U
	O T T I
	T L B T

Trace it and write it

Color the picture and fill in the missing letter

_iger

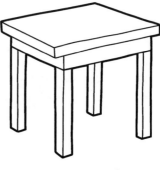

_able

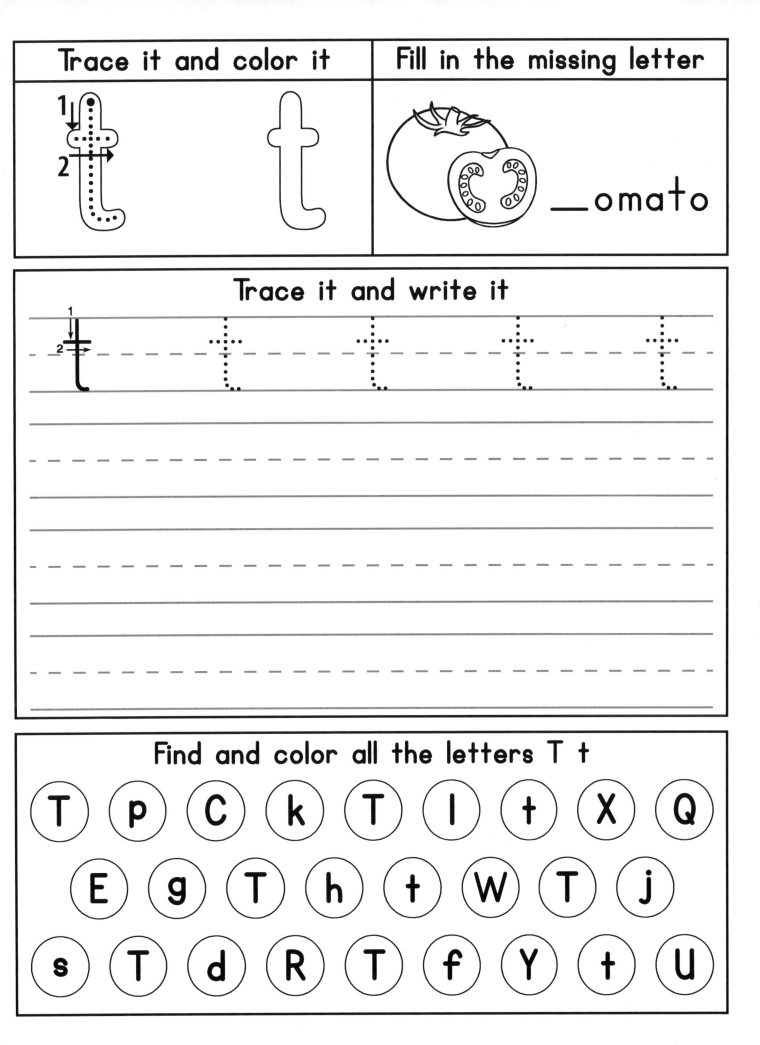

Trace it and color it	Circle it
	U I U V N U U W U V Z U

Trace it and write it

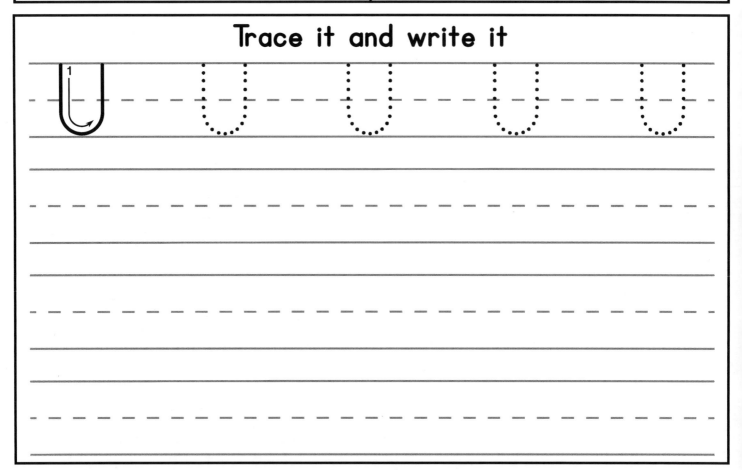

Color the picture and fill in the missing letter

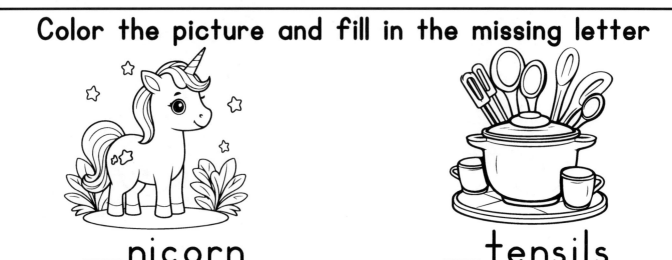

_nicorn   _tensils

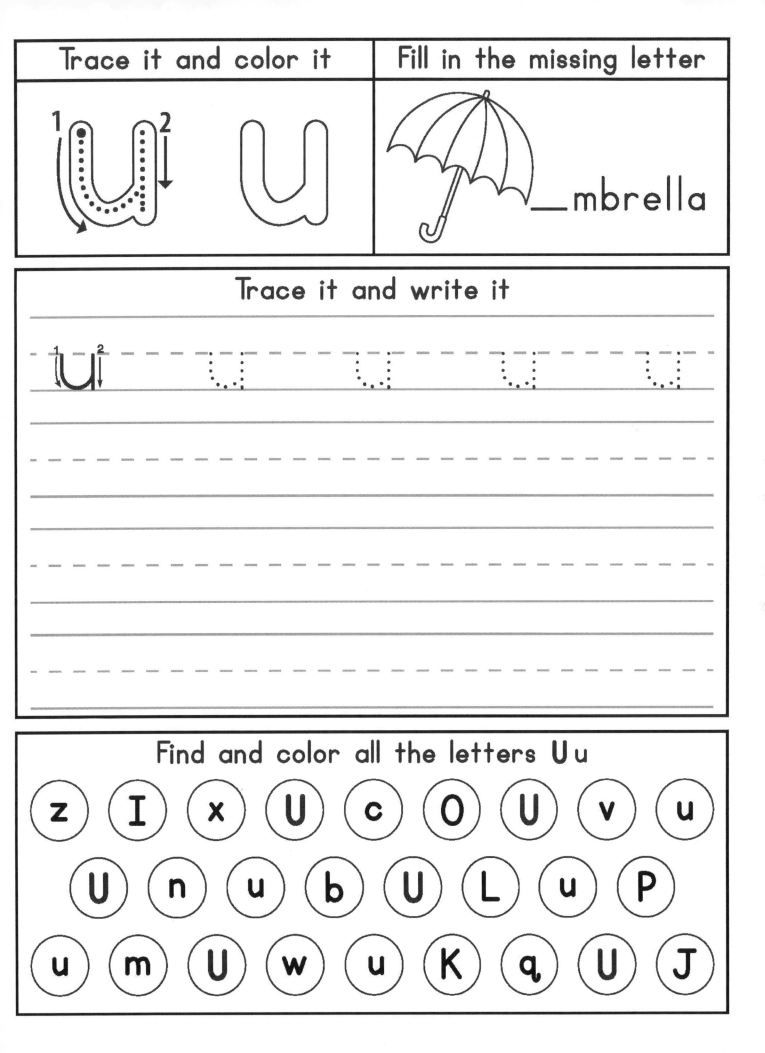

Trace it and color it

Circle it

W	V	N	V
A	G	V	Y
V	S	L	V

Trace it and write it

Color the picture and fill in the missing letter

__iolin

__olcano

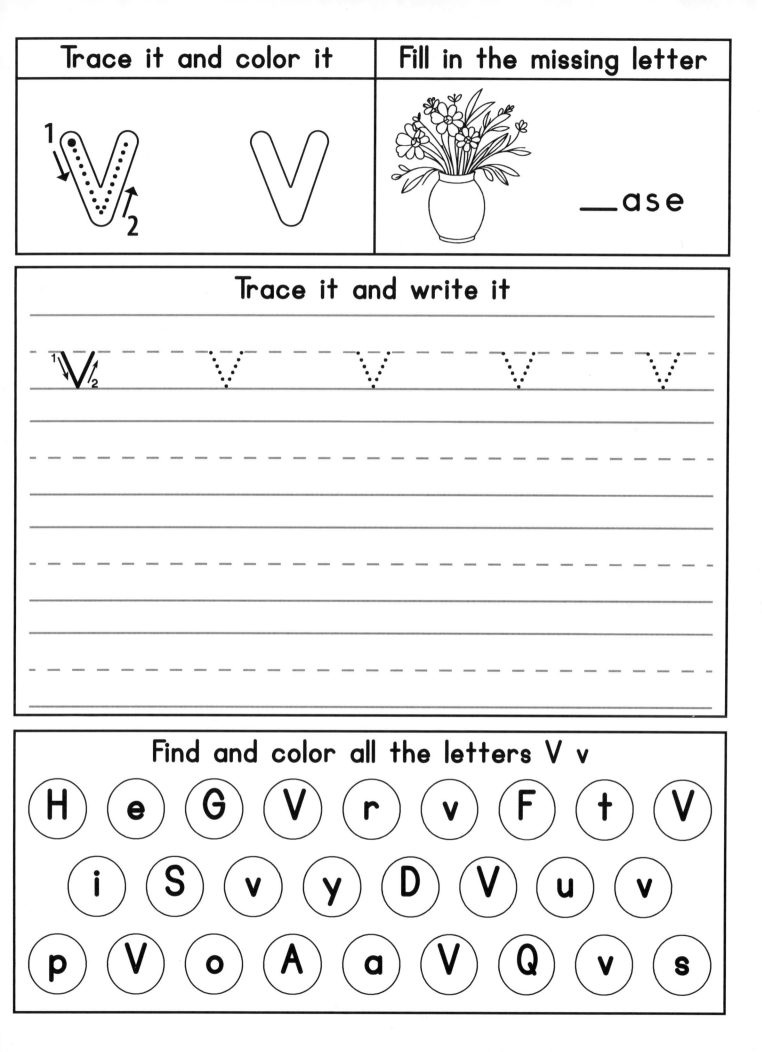

Trace it and color it	Circle it
	A V W H E W M W W N W K

Trace it and write it

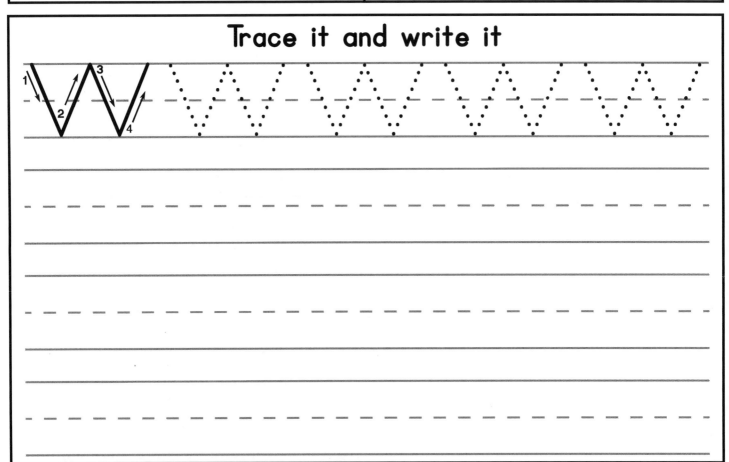

Color the picture and fill in the missing letter

_eb

_indow

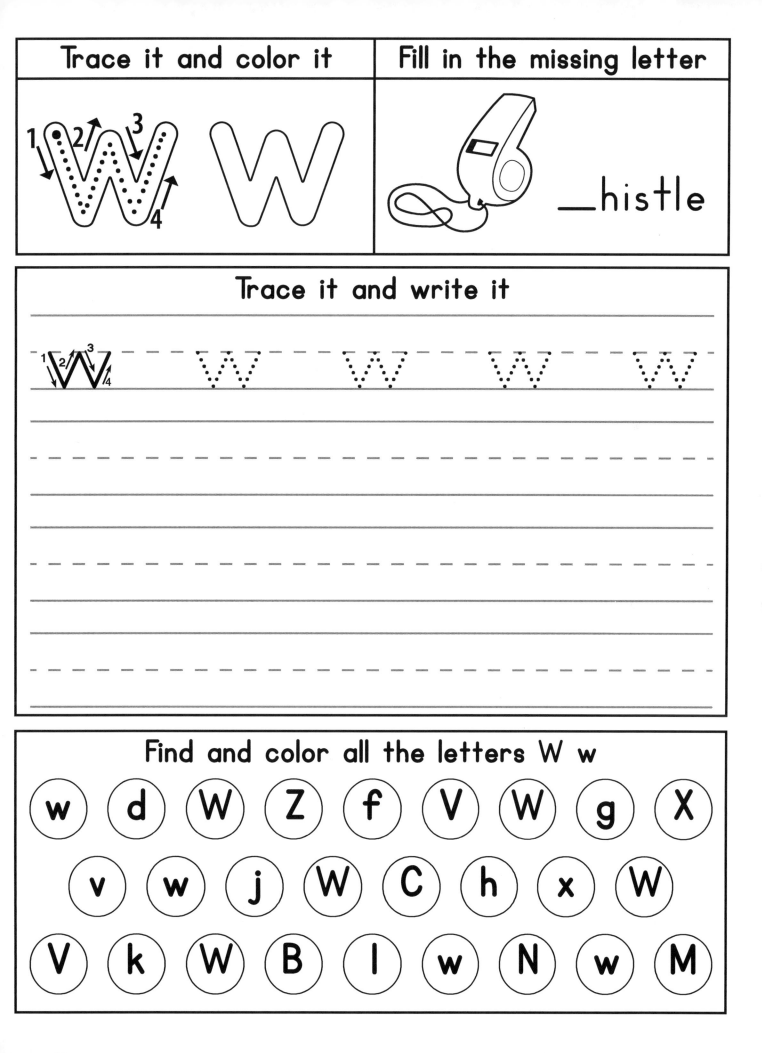

Trace it and color it

Circle it

X	Y	Z	X
T	X	X	S
X	H	L	X

Trace it and write it

Color the picture and fill in the missing letter

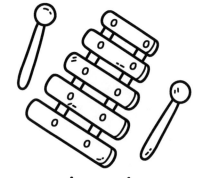

__ylophone

__mas tree

Trace it and color it

Circle it

V	Y	Y	N
Y	F	Y	K
T	Y	C	I

Trace it and write it

Color the picture and fill in the missing letter

___acht

___oga

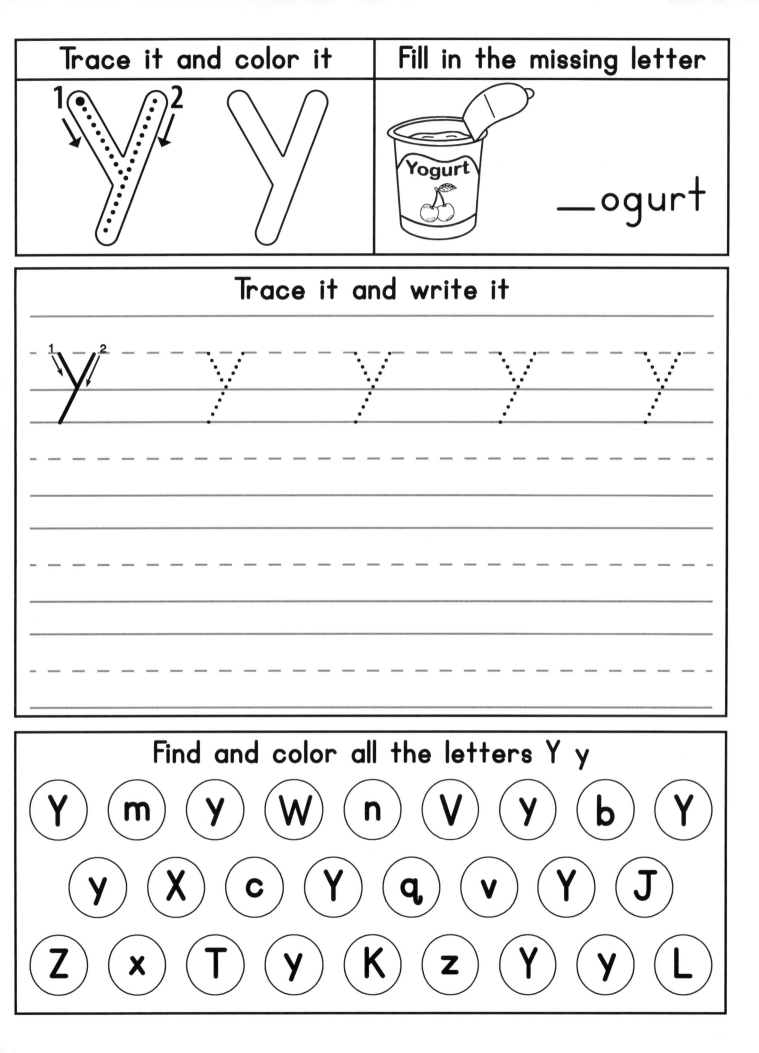

Trace it and color it	Circle it
	Z W Z N K Z H Z Z M Z R

Trace it and write it

Color the picture and fill in the missing letter

_ebra

_oo

Trace it and color it

Fill in the missing letter

___ipper

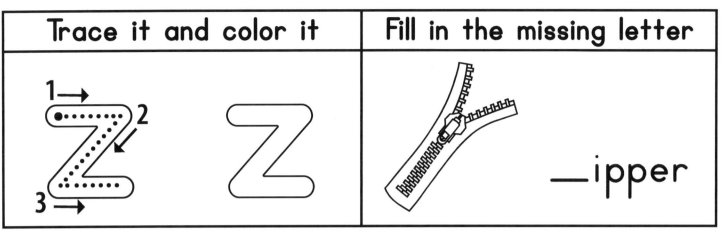

Trace it and write it

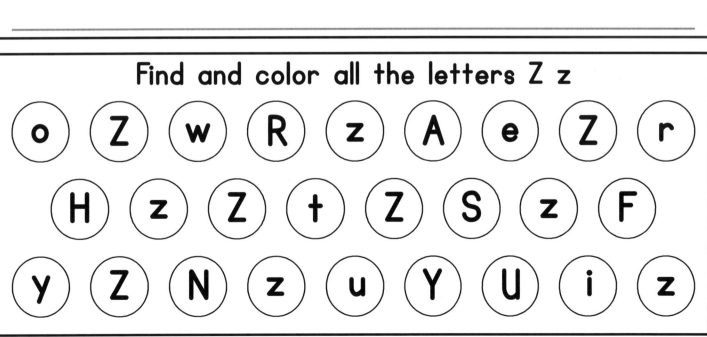

Find and color all the letters Z z

We value our customers and always welcome your **feedback** and suggestions. If you have enjoyed this book or any other titles from our range please consider leaving an honest **review** on **Amazon**.

Thank you!

Amazon.com   **Amazon.co.uk**

Made in the USA
Middletown, DE
08 February 2025

71013421R00031